<u>Robbed by</u>

<u>My Depression</u>

<u>*Author RJLB*</u>

Intro

Merely you only adapt to

what your environment

is, but if you've never

had an opportunity to

know your natural

environment you must

survive to what is known.

When God gives you life,

you live; God gives you

sight, you look to

brighter days; But when

God gives you love, take

it and never look back.

Throughout life I've been

a child seen by many as

weird or strange but in a

sense you fear what you

don't know or

understand. I've just

been myself that's it.

Many youth and young

adults tend to want to

portray a role that may

allow progress or create

a hindrance. And I must

say I wouldn't find it

technically in someone's

best interest to become

anyone but themselves.

Over the course of my

life I've been a musician

and artist, but I haven't

had any circumstances

in which I have judged or

persecuted anyone. I

just realized that life isn't

about your circumstance

but it is about the

direction best for the

individual. My family, I

always see them from

time to time but most of

the time I am either

occupying my time either

reading, writing or

drawing pictures.

Five signs of Mental Illness

- <u>Worry</u>

- <u>Grumpiness</u>

- <u>Isolation</u>

- <u>Different Sleep Patterns</u>

- <u>Melancholy</u>

Letter to Momma:

Dear Momma,

As I am sitting in this

cell, I wish life would've

been different for me. I

apologize for what

happened that day. I

truly don't remember

what happened and I am

honestly sorry. I wish I

could tell the guy, but my

mind wasn't right. I go to

sleep every night praying

I can get another chance

at life because these

four walls aren't my

resident. Schedule to

eat on their time,

sleeping on a timed

schedule, not being able

to enjoy life only fun is

playing chess or working

out. I know I need help

for this blackouts I have.

Why would I ever hurt

someone is the question

I ask myself each day.

Hopefully I can find out

the reason before it is

too late. They've set me

up with a therapist but

every time I see her I'm

in shackles each visit.

But when we talk she's

nice and she has made

me feel that the only

thing is that I've been

battling with a mental

illness for about a year

now. So I pray she can

help me also with the

help of God. I love you

momma. And I hope to

see you soon.

Love your Son,

RJ

Cold Turkey

You're probably

wondering why I feel

this way. Well it all

started one day I was

smoking the best bud

in the city, and this

time it had me higher

than a mountain goat

climbing a hill.

Overthinking and

paranoid and these

were things I didn't

usually feel after a fat

Dutch Master rolled

blunt, but I was lost. I

was just in a state of

mind of fear. The first

sign of Worry

approaching me. Deep

breath after, deep

breath I was slowing

falling into a feel I

couldn't express. So I

just went to my dorm

room and slept it

off......Usually I'm

hanging with my girl at

the time chilling but

I'm just chilling up

playing the ps3. It was

that PS3 that could

play Ps1 and Ps2 disc

all on one console. Was

an amazing thing in my

life it really allowed me

to see the world and

how it changes daily

and yearly; all the

different games from

generations of

Playstation media I had

a variety of games that

got me through my

many college days.. It's

about 12:30 a.m. I

wake up... Yawn, class

at 8:30 a.m. but I feel

like someone's

watching me.....I was

just dreaming I didn't

notice this but it's like

a daydream before you

wake up just showing

me some foresight for

the day. But it's just

another anxiety attack.

But I don't really know

why these things are

happening. BOOM! I

lay back down it's

already 5:45 a.m. so I

can slide a quick nap in

but this time, I can't

sleep I was totally

grumpy. Couldn't even

lay down without

jumping back up afraid

I'll over sleep but that's

how all college

students felt some

days. But who am I

kidding I'll just have to

go cold turkey for a

while.

Fast forward day three of

cold turkey, I've slept a

total of 9 hours because

I only get good sleep

when I smoke. My whole

demeanor has changed.

I would usually wake up

get Mississippi pimp

smooth and try and take

a dude girl. I say that

because it's "Just Me",

but today I'm feeling

bummish. Walking

around campus a beanie,

long sleeved shirt,

shorts, long socks and

some crocs. But peep

game the females still

jocking but I was so lost

in myself at that time I

didn't indulge. First sign

of me changing.

A couple of days go

by and I'm stressed me

and my girl arguing life

ain't going my way. I'm

broke, but I can pay for a

gram of loud with ease. I

didn't have my priorities

straight and it showed.

She nagged and nagged but deep down she knew mentally something was wrong. She was potentially sometime a trigger at times. And at time we didn't see eye to eye, but I loved her and *nothing mattered.   So*

one day an argument

reached its peak and I

wanted space but I was

so stuck in my

depression I texted her

and said "The world

would definitely be

better without me." That

was the depression and

it scared her so bad she

called my family and the

campus police. They

were there in a flash. I'm

folding up clothes then I

hear a key jiggling in my

door and it was all the

campus police and the

hall director asking,

"Was I fine and did I have

a gun or weapon I could

harm myself with?" I

politely denied them and

I felt betrayed because I

didn't think nothing of

the message but at that

point in time she knew I

wasn't the same person

at the time. So my family

made it to me in less

than an hour, versus the

normal amount of time of

the trip is about 1 hour

and 45 mins tops. So

they make it not knowing

I'm actually pissed now

because they think I'm

going through a mid-life

crysys. Free Typo☺

But in all realness I

believe that moment was

a mid-life crisis. So I was

soon packing up my stuff

so that I could move

back home due to my

first encounter of me

getting "Robbed by my

Depression." Mind you

I'm back home now but

I'm starting to show

signs of Isolation. At

the same time I rarely

get out because I only

hang out with my family,

Tymira or my Brother

Trey. But now I rarely

spend time with my

family, Tymira or my

brother, that's when I

knew I wasn't myself

anymore. I started

missing church, I started

driving to destinations I

didn't think to go, and I

was merely an idol mind

trying to find myself

throughout this

depressive state of mind.

So Tymira was my

girlfriend and she helped

me through many of days

in my college life and I

appreciate her for

everything she did for me

at my lowest in my life

years back. I thank you.

And my Brother Trey, he

was there every step of

the way being a pinnacle

in my life to remember."

you got me bro, we out

here praying and praying

for you bro" I could hear

that from one of the

visits we were on and it

stuck with me. I'm

thankful for you bro.

You can lose your Life

One day I'm minding my

business waiting to buy a

1/8th so this day in

particular two guys walk

up, Jay and DeeDee,

token "not actual names"

I had previous given

them a blunt. And they

were coming to ask a

question I could see it in

their eyes.

Motherfucking Jay gone

ask me "Big bro if you

about to smoke can we

roll with you?" My

response "Naw this a

single man mission right

here."

I said that because all I

see them doing every

day is asking for change

for a square or picking

up old 1roaches or

cigarettes people didn't

finish.

So my plug finally pulls

up and I'm moving fast

and I leave my phone on

the picnic table they

---

[1] Roaches: end of Blunt

were sitting at. Cool. I

walk back and Jay asked

me one more time. "Aye

big bro can me and

DeeDee smoke with

you?" and I just said

"Nah" not knowing Jay

has put my phone is his

pocket. So I walk off on

my daily smoke session

by myself and midway

rolling up it hit me I

couldn't find my phone.

So I'm about 1000 steps

away but I'm pearling

this blunt and I wasn't in

any type of rush because

I'm about to be baked

like a potato. I get

finished and walked back

to my previous

destination. So Jay, who

was the prime suspect

sitting by his self. So I

approached him, I'm high

so I'm just ultimately

chilled. I asked "Aye did

you see my phone?" Jay

replies "I ain't seen your

phone big bro but I just

sold mine for some Ice."

So I'm puzzled and high

because I know Ice a

crackhead drug and

people would do

anything for a fix. So I

say "So you didn't see

my phone?" he stated

again, "Nah but I just

sold mine for some Ice, it

had text messages,

internet all that good shit

on it." So I blew my high

simultaneously and I'm

on go mode now because

I feel like this crack head

ass little boy just sold my

phone for some Ice. I

started pacing the

pavement because I'm

ready to beat dude ass,

but I can't do nothing

where I'm at because it's

too risky. I state to him

"I aint got nothing to lose

so give me that phone

back." Before I tell you

his response this where I

mentally lose my

composure I turned into

the person I keep bottled

up. Pretty much like my

incredible Hulk side.

Where I can control

myself because I'll

blackout. So then Jay

stated, "You do have

something to lose." I say

"What?" Each word

verbatim "You can lose

your Life!" So now I can

go to my room and get

the pistol and tell God

you got somebody on the

way to see you, but then

I thought to myself that

phone had major

numbers like plugs and

family. And now he's the

only one to have it or

sold it to someone and

the issue arise they

know exactly who did it.

So I blow off my steam

and walked it off. Every

move I make is a chess

move, but sometimes I

revert back to checker

moves when my mind

goes blank. This would

be the first time that I

had an experience to

make me drift

consciously into a place

I couldn't leave. A place

I call "Blacking Out."

Blacking out is a place I

can't control, I mentally

and physically tune out

and I can't control

myself. Pretty much a

Hulk like state of mind.

All that happened in a

course of about 15

minutes. Mind you I'm a

nice and considerate

person but these are

situations where I can't

control myself. It just

feels as if I can't control

myself, but I'm the pilot

of my ship I have to

control it and bottle it up.

Mindset

I've encountered a lot of things and no will ever know me because I'm a chess man. Every move you think you are making towards me only leads to you being put in checkmate within 5

moves in my mental

mind, consciously. Most

of the time I am speaking

to people subconsciously

due to me not wanting to

show people

intentionally how smart I

am. No one needs to

know how smart you are

because reading the

back of a book only tells

you a snippet versus

starting from page one

learning and

understanding the book.

So you won't understand

me unless I open up to

you and only my family

and Tymira and Trey

know me. I tend to do

this because I want to

know you as a person

how you move, how you

act, your intentions this

allows me to evaluate

you each day like I'm a

Psychiatrist. You'll never

know when you're

entertaining an Angel of

God so you should

always be on your toes

when meeting people.

I'm not an Angel either.

So either you are a friend

or foe regardless I won't

be around to allow you to

understand me. This

book here is to help

people with mental

illness this is the closes

I'll ever let a person get

to know me. So if you

know me from this book

you don't, I just want to

help you get further like I

have. "I go harder

because I know where I

was at and now I know

where I want to go."

Future said that in "Kno

the Meaning."

The Reason Why

So I know you're

wondering why I was in

jail. I have no

recollection on why it

happened but I was

mentally lost at the time.

I didn't know myself

anymore. And I use to be

upset for no apparent

reason. I just knew I

wasn't the same

anymore. It was a

beautiful day everything

was going well. I woke

up and got ready to go to

school a Community

college trying to finish

and pursue my dream of

being a multi-billion

dollar business manager.

Day goes well as

expected but today I was

uneven. A couple of

days before I asked my

mother if I could get

help, I felt I needed

therapy because I was

mentally over

capacitated with the 5

Signs of Mental Illness

- *Worry was shown when I got to school I was feeling like I was being watched and followed so I kept a knife on me.*

- *Grumpiness was very much seen because I*

was awake about a

good 36 hours after

telling my mother I

needed help. It was

serious now.

- Isolation I spoke to

people but I was

much so like the

black sheep of my

classes and on

campus but I knew

so many people and

they couldn't tell by

the way I moved.

Meaning how I was

so happy and

energetic.

- *Different Sleep*

 Patterns I didn't

 sleep so I was in a

 dramatic situation

 from not sleeping for

 about 2 days.

Another sign of

needing help.

- *Melancholy now here*

this is extremely the

one you need to

watch out for

because I was happy

one minute and soon

after I was in rage

type of feel if you

looked at me wrong.

So I finish my class day

and I walk to my

mother's job. Told her

I wanted to exercise

when in reality I'm

already fit I weighed

about 185 solid. So I

make it there and I

hang out for a while

then I asked her could

say "What's up" to my

cousin. I make it there

and I'm alright but

something took over

me. I blacked out. I had

sipped, maybe drank 2

coronas and what

happened next

changed my whole life

forever. I stabbed a

man in his neck;

mentally, physically

and emotionally I was

not R.J. at the moment.

I tried remembering

why it happened but I

don't remember

anything. When I

awoke from my black

out there was blood on

me and I had my knife

in my hand. So I'm

scared I run to the

closest vehicle to me

wanting to figure out

what had just

happened. So I get

into a work truck, and

before I knew it was a

police officer pointing

his barrel directly in my

face. My life flashed

before my eyes.

Birthdays, missed

loved ones just visuals

that were in my

conscious mind. So I

look out the window

another one of my

cousins just says, "RJ

just put your hands

up." And I listened.

The cop pulled me out

and handcuffed me.

When I say I was in a

place of disbelief

because I just see

blood and a knife.

They place me in the

Suburban and within a

flash people were

everywhere. My family

and family friends are

there wanting to know

what happened. From

inside of the truck I

see my mother pull up

and they told her what

happened. She

instantly fell out. And

then I felt the

extremity of what

happened. They took

me to the police

station for questioning

and the police officer

was nice but I was

definitely fucked up in

the head at this point.

She asked, "Do you

know what happened,

Sir?" I tell her I don't

remember and I was

serious. I sat for about

an hour maybe less.

And then I was

transported to the

County Jail on a charge

of 1st Degree Battery.

First Day

My first day there they

put me in a holding cell

by myself for about 3

days and it felt like 20

days. They booked me

and I'm still mentally

fucked, they asked

where was I born and I

stated "Santo Domingo,

Dominican Republic"

and I knew that wasn't

a conscious decision

on my behalf. My mind

was horrible and it was

reconstructed for being

locked up for that

amount of time. My

first hearing the judge

asked me "Was I okay

and did I remember

what happened?" I

stated no. My mom

and dad were there and

he said your son needs

help and I'll set his

bond high so he can

receive the rehab he

needs. The judge said

your son bond is

$500,000. Next Cases.

I looked and my heart

dropped but I needed

help. But I know that's

definitely a lot of

money. So my time

there I received rehab

from inmates and

therapist. They had me

on a prescription

because they deemed

me schizophrenic.

They stated that the

episode was a dormant

schizophrenic illness.

That was there and

was so extreme it

could've placed me in

jail for a long time. But

while in jail my rehab

with the other inmates

was playing chess for

my mind to think better

under pressure and

reading various books

to expand my mind as

well. But the story

doesn't stop there. I

spent 2 months in a

Mental Hospital for

them to figure out the

best option for me.

State Hospital

My psychiatrist was

very weird from the

start. She told me in

one of my sessions in

front of everyone. "Do

you feel like you'll be

able to live in a locked

facility for 5 years

when you get on

probation?" But the

head doctor already

had spoken with me

about the options

depending on my well-

being. It was either go

to a locked facility or

do the probation from

home. So I told the

lady I'll be your first

person to do probation

from home. She got so

upset to the point it

seemed like she was

betting money I would

be in a locked facility.

One thing about a child

of God you can't do

them wrong because

God has a protective

shield around them.

And he also stated

Vengeance is mine.

The same lady lost her

license because she

escaped a person from

the state hospital and

wanted to start a life

with him. This

happened the same

day I was released

home. It's amazing

how God works in your

favor. I didn't ever

leave him behind when

I was up nor while I

was down. I especially

needed him during this

crisis. I slept on my

bible in jail and at the

state hospital because

I wanted God on my

mind going to sleep,

while I was sleep and

as soon as I woke up.

Day Treatment

So now I'm at home, no

job, no money, or

nothing. I had to

restart life. I have

freedom to drive, well

not yet had to renew

my license and they

didn't want to up and

start back driving off

the rip. Another key

component though with

the probation I had to

go through Day

Treatment. Meaning I

had to go to a mental

health facility daily for

rehab and learn more

info of my mental

illness so I don't

relapse. Relapse is

when an issue or even

more extreme than

your other

mental/psychotic

episode happens again.

And I vowed that I

wouldn't ever happen

again. So I start day

treatment and I get a

therapist she didn't

read my file and the

first thing she stated to

me, "You're a rapist

right?" I damn near

slapped that lady ass

for disrespecting me,

but I politely stated

back, "No ma'am but

did you read my file?"

She said, "no but I

need to read it now for

the mishap." While I

was there she tried

provoking me often

with reverse

psychology but it didn't

work because my mind

doesn't pick up on

stupidity nor people

who try to slander my

image for their own

liking. I stayed in a

day treatment about a

year and I got a job at

FedEx. I had to give

out my probation

papers but it all worked

out. I worked there

about 10 months, I put

a down payment of a

car and I was happy for

that. I took on the

responsibilities I

should've took on way

earlier but smoking

was an expensive habit

I had back then. Now I

have a way better job

and I'm months from

being off of probation.

I've worked diligently

and steady to get back

to the freedom of

travelling whenever,

going out the country,

buying a house

because with the

probation I had to stay

with family to make

sure I followed up on

my probation and stuck

to it. I am beyond

blessed and I just want

to tell you if you have

any of these symptoms

don't fight it seek a

therapist. That'll be

the best decision you'll

make in your life. The

first thing I was told at

the State Hospital is

that Artist, Lawyers,

Doctors and a hand full

of people take

antipsychotics

because they battle

with the same issues

you face. You're

definitely not alone. So

remember the <u>5 Signs</u>

<u>of Mental Illness.</u>

- Worry

- Grumpiness

- Isolation

- Different Sleep

  Patens

- Melancholy

You should very much

seek help because life

can change in the blink

of an eye.

Finale

I enjoy my life because

God took me on a

journey that has changed

me into such a strong

man that I look over

people because I refuse

to blackout or ever

relapse over no stupidity.

Nevertheless there is

always an obstacle on

your course no matter

how sane you are. It

takes a very insane

person to stay sane in

this world. It get crazier

every day. Kids toting

guns like they soldiers,

adults fighting kids due

to lack of respect for one

another; we just need to

slow down and look at

the bigger picture. We

the people, we are all we

got. If you know God

then you know you're

believing in someone you

haven't seen, talked to,

or even touched. But

trust me God is very real

so start believing and

trusting in him more.

You believe in him but

you can't believe in the

next person? But I get it

people are very

conniving and hard to

trust, but God put us

here for a purpose. So

work each day striving to

find that reason. YOUR

PURPOSE!